the chambered nautilus

the chambered nautilus

allan barr

Thistledown Press Ltd.

Canadian Cataloguing in Publication Data

Barr, Allan, 1959-

The chambered nautilus

(New leaf editions)
Poems.
ISBN 0-920633-93-5

I. Title. II. Series.

PS8553.A77C43 1992   C811'.54   C92-098076-7
PR199.3.B37C43   1992

Book design by A.M. Forrie
Cover drawing by Jane Bannon, paper by Tanya Norman
Typeset by Thistledown Press Ltd.

Printed and bound in Canada by
Kromar Printing Ltd.
725 Portage Ave.
Winnipeg, MB   R3G 0M8

Thistledown Press Ltd.
668 East Place
Saskatoon, Saskatchewan   S7J 2Z5

Acknowledgements

The Adrienne Rich quotation is from "Poem of Women", adapted from a
Yiddish poem by Kadia Molodovsky. It appears in *The Fact of a Doorframe*
(W.W. Norton & Company, New York, 1984).
The Tom Berryman quotations are from "76 Henry's Confession", which
appeared in *77 Dream Songs* (Farrar, Straus and Giroux, New York, 1964).

Some of these poems have appeared or will soon appear in: *Antigonish
Review*, *Blue Streak in a Dry Year* (Saskatoon Poets Coterie, 1980),
Fiddlehead, *FreeLance*, *Grain*, *Heading Out* (Coteau Books, 1986), *Minus
Tides*, *New Quarterly*, *Pierian Spring*, *Secrets from the Orange Couch*, and
Waves.

This book has been published with the assistance of The Canada Council
and the Saskatchewan Arts Board.

CONTENTS

I

II

The wind comes around the house
as though you are inside a seashell,
in the centre of the roaring sound you hear
when you put your ear against it.
Like your heart the shell is funnelled
and secret, its axis hidden. You could stay
a hundred years in its chambers.
No one would find you.

In the kitchen your husband's boots
leave black knots of mud on the linoleum.
You hate the sound of the chair legs
scraping the floor when he sits,
the liquid sound of his drinking.

If he goes you will dance
to whatever song the radio plays.
You will turn on the television and dance
naked in the blue light, your breasts
and buttocks will shine, your hands
will flutter in the blue.

His bottle will be empty soon.
The wind has stopped and the stillness
makes you think it must be evening.
In your chamber it is always dark
and silent. You cannot hear his drinking
or his boots on the floor, you cannot hear
your blood moving or the roaring
he would hear if he listened
to the shell's lip. You are inside
the roaring and it comes from you.

                      are the timbers
of a burning house, blackened by fire, breaking
your skin as they fall. You try to drag them whole
from the gutted centre of your language,
try to pull the beams and studs
and crumbling joists from their beds
like smoke-strangled children.
They turn to ashes in your hands, your skin
bubbles like blistering paint.

Afterward you will paint stones
with the ashes and carry them in your pocket,
you will rub them together, your fingers
will come away blackened.

He was an old man when his dog died.
Even half-starved
it was huge, its scapulae
like shovel blades. Harry
dug until he couldn't breathe
but it wasn't enough.

There was too much dog left
for the hole he'd made, too little man
for the work. He made it fit.
I saw him by the grave in his backyard
with a kindling maul in his hand
breaking the bones like sticks.

                        lives in a storm of falling glass, chiming
as it shatters around his feet. He spends hours some days
picking the glass out of his bloody socks. He doesn't know
how things began to slip out of his hands. He is surrounded
by windows, anyone can see him. When it rains the whole house rings.
This old man he plays the string bass on his suspenders
for diversion, he juggles balls of glass that hail about his head,
he waits for the day he will fall, ringing like crystal,
the length of his shortening shadow. On days when the light
cuts through his windows and pins him there, in his familiar
storm-bound, clattering rooms, he holds his bloody feet in his hands
and will not pray for deliverance.

Now it's one thirty-seven. Eight.
Nine. Count it off.

Anyway it's late. A black dog
rolls my neighbour's silver trash can

like thunder down the road. One night
about this time I saw a man naked

under his bathrobe running
down Fourth Street. Five. Six. I'm drunk

and I was drunk, I know, when I saw him
in my headlights. But those white

naked feet running in the new snow!

My heart cannons against my ribs. I reach for my watch.
I don't know what I think it can tell me.
I stare around in the dark, trying to decide
how much of this is real and what's still dream:

the green streetlamp light bleeding in
through the curtain, the unquestionable presence
of your body beside me, asleep, mute and heavy
as a slab of meat,
                          this moment after every beat
when my heart stops
                   then starts again.

I wake up at four a.m. and the streets
are pounding with black water, rain
crashing out of the black night.

From our bedroom window I see wolves
moving in the streets.
The bolder ones stop to lap from the gutters,
eat cats and foul the tidy lawns.
Sharks cruise out of manholes, looking
for milkmen or poodles on long leashes.
Clouds of vultures converge
to sort the dead and the living. Which are you,
asleep there?

Black rain batters the church bells,
crows explode from steeples
and head south. Everywhere
the world gets on with its business,
moving and eating and fucking.

You sleep like some carcass. God
help me, I'll cut my throat before I tell you
even once more that I love you.

I wasn't talking. The bartender
took away the glasses as soon as they were empty.
I wasn't talking, he could see that. A woman came in,
a fight started, a bomb went off, the ceiling
fell, a war began and ended. I went on drinking.
He went on pouring. Don't worry he said.
This happens all the time. You don't have to say
a word.

The place was full of survivors, like it or not
they'd all pull through. There was a girl
with half her foot shot off, a man
walking around with his sleeves full of blood,
a little boy getting his lip stitched. The black
thread dragging through his skin.

One man they said had smashed through
the window of a burning house and fallen
two floors to the sidewalk
with his clothes on fire. He'd live.

I knelt by his cot to see him better.
Blood from under my cuffs trailed down
my palm and dripped off my fingertips.
I'd have sworn he was still burning
the way his body shone.

The delicate white bones of a fish
gleam underwater among rushes and shells.
She takes them home in her pocket,
sets them above the stove to dry
like wishbones.

　　　　　When they are ready,
she casts them on a red-and-black silk scarf
to read her future. The jawbones
mate in a horrible fish grin. She tries
to grind them to powder but the stone pestle
splits in her hand, reveals
the fossilized traces
of a sharp-toothed fish.

　　　　　That night
translucent red fish rise as from a great depth
to her bed, glow above her
in the silky black of her sleep.

the train's hiss
tongues the old man's ear
    he fumbles free of his soiled blanket
like a man waking in his bath
finding his mouth choked with water

and as the passengers leave the train
and move down the tiled platform
he begins to shout   to fill the stale air
with the palsied language
of his body
    the shout spirals down the tunnel
twisting   until every spine
feels its knuckled touch

the train moves off
pushing the dry air in front of it
    riding the live rail
      into darkness

from the underground platform
into the tiled   elbow-bent corridors
   my footsteps clatter
in the close sweaty air   my hands
pale in the harsh light
   through the escalator tunnel
I ascend toward street level
into a grey   artificial twilight
   at the turnstiles
it is interior evening   but beyond
the cashiers' cages the day
presses down on the pavements
   just past the exit
a photographer   joined to his tripod
by slender white hands
   framed by the darkness behind
I step through the door   into day
as the flashbulb detonates
   my body explodes with light

1

In the garden the boys are laughing,
they are running and leaping and the wind
leaps with them through the dry
leaves and through the tangled garden.

The women of the house watch
from back rooms where the air
is stale and close with mourning
and the musk of desire. They watch
the boys, their flashing limbs,
the sweat and sunlight that glint
in their flowing hair. And the Duke
alone in his upstairs room
sees the boys leaping with the wind,
moving inside their clothing
as though they might at any moment
fly free of it, and he thinks
of the widows in their closed rooms
swaying inside their mourning gowns
like breeze through the dark curtains,
and O the mystery O the beautiful
buttocks of the women, the hidden
flowers of their sex, the smells
in the downstairs rooms of lotions
and powders and sweat and the sour
woman smell that tugs at his groin.

In the garden the boys
are leaping over rusted lawn mowers
and cracked red flowerpots
and the red tooth of the abandoned scythe.

2

On their red bicycles the boys
fly through the garden, under the eyes
of their uncle the crookback Duke.

Winter is coming, he feels it
in his bent spine. The boys
trouble his thoughts. He has examined
his conscience and found
he loves them not, nor the women
who moan and curse in their rooms below.

In their natures there is something
that offends him, like the smell of sex,
the sharp sweet stink of the honeysuckle
in his rotting garden.

3

This is a house of women,
of bitter words and the angry
desire of widowhood. From their rooms below
he hears the voices of women
poisoning the boys against him.

Beware of the scythe, they say, beware
of your uncle the mad Duke,
the crooked Duke, beware of his bent spine
and his black eyes, the lank hair
that hangs on his head like the weeds
of his garden. Under his rags
he is a running sore, under his skull
he is the garden, untended, left
to rot and freeze in the ground.

He hears the boys, in their voices the sweetness
and gentleness of their youth. They sing
to him, O the beautiful boys:
Mad Uncle Richard, stinky Uncle Richard
He sweats and he farts and he snorts
He sucks his thumb and he picks his bum
And he sniffs at the crotch of his shorts

The air in the house is foul,
it stinks of the talk of women.
The house is riven and all
conspire against him. Adjustments
will be made, there will be
no sedition in this house, peace
of a sort will be made.

4

Anarchy, anarchy, his anthem:
let earth sweat bile
from its filthy pores, let the flower
of benevolence be torn at the root,
let rank weeds overwhelm the garden.

He has been too patient
with the lying lustful women,
with the shameless boys
and O their sweet cloying voices.
Now his fists will stop the lewd
mouths of the women, his hands
bind the boys and hide from the eye
their naked insolent limbs.

Let chaos sport, lovers
infect each other, the garden muck
squelch and suck at shameless flesh,
the scythe's fang loose its venom.

Let the heavens open and the skies
piss down their benediction
on the rotting world.

sitting   precisely
still   awake   or not
awake   in the middle
of a room full of books
and suitcases
reading about someone
else's life

mormons   witnesses
do not come
to my door   no one
comes to my door
apparently I do not
require salvation

the howling of wolves
and down the road
dogs answer
sharply   the cat
hides between my feet

two deer
slip by the window
quiet as prayer

Throw a whole forest in the firebox:
nothing warms this house.

We sit with blankets around our shoulders,
feet on the grate, and still

can't keep out the old cold memories,
the chill, unkind, divorcing night.

Like wind the world keeps rolling in
under our doors.

I'm only hanging on here. Lately the floorboards
have been moving. At night I hear them
stretching and creaking, testing their nails.

We're making ready for departure, the floor and I.
If I don't get out first I'll probably fall through
and spend the rest of my life in the cellar.

Already there are gaps in the floor. The carpets sag.
This is just a note to say I'm leaving,
one piece at a time.

There's a cross-country line now
between us. From two hundred miles
I feel you sparking and firing,
arcing blue in the green night.

You say when I see you again
it won't be like the last time,
when you were drunk and wanted me.
But I'm crackling down the wires

underground and over the crossarms
of power poles to where you are
sleeping and tonight I'll blow out
your fuses and burn your house down.

We've gotten away with it. Tonight
I'll go back to my lawfully wedded, you
to yours and your horrible children.
Nobody's found us out, the police
are not coming for us. Lawyers
with ugly photographs and their black
hearts showing aren't coming for us.

How can we live without
each other, we say, and how
can we go on like this. It's not right.
We have responsibilities to others.
This has to end, now.

I watch you drive away.
When you turn the corner
I decide to put my cap on
sideways. Dance a little dance.
Whistle a little tune.

I'm sitting at a table in a bar downtown.
My friend Steve is sitting across from me.
He's holding my right hand with both of his and he's
    crying.
He thinks his wife is sleeping with somebody.
People keep looking at us like we're in the wrong kind
    of bar.

My lover tells me I'm afraid of intimacy.
She says intimacy is a beautiful thing.
She says when you're really intimate with somebody you
    can tell everything he thinks and feels just by
    touching him.
She wishes I would learn to trust her.

I wish Steve would stop crying and let go of my hand.
It's not that I'm afraid of intimacy.
It's not that I care what the people in the bar think
    when they look at us touching like that.
Steve's right.
Someone is sleeping with his wife.
I wish he'd let go of my hand.

For months now I've been busy all day not smoking.
I watch TV or work at my desk and never smoke all the time.
After work I go for walks, when I get back this woman
I'm living with now asks me where I've been.
I tell her I've been out, not smoking every step of the way.

Sometimes I go out in the evening and things happen,
they just happen, they happen to me and there's nothing
I can do about it. I have a few drinks and no cigarettes
and things happen that I can't write down in case this woman
that I'm living with now finds this.

I've got poems and notes, descriptions of the things
that happen to me, hidden all over the house,
just like a woman I knew kept cigarettes
and matches stashed around her house
when she told people she wasn't smoking.

I lie in bed all night and don't smoke. Sometimes
I dream that this woman I'm living with now
is lying on the floor and I'm standing over her yelling
what do you want, can't you see
how hard this is? Still
not smoking.

He sits and drinks or plays pool and drinks
or dances and drinks between songs
and is happy. His friends drain
pitchers of beer, claim the pool table
and the dance floor as their own.
Nothing is safe from them.

He is happy. He will not qualify that
yet. There are three women here
he'd like to sleep with, more
as the night goes on. He is happy for now.
He drinks another beer, dances
with another woman, blows another
game of pool. He is happy.
He swears he is.

It's only seven goddamn degrees below
zero and the goddamn thing won't turn over.
The choke linkage's buggered, the battery's
buggered, the goddamn electrical system's
buggered buggered buggered.

I'd like to live someplace warmer. I'd like
a few dozen bottles of decent wine,
a hundred extra bucks a month, a thousand
and one nights in Arabia, a million things.
I'd like a car that runs, a different job
or no job at all, a new wife, a new life.

(Sitting in the dark at seven below
in a car that won't run and isn't
goddamn paid for.)

Most Friday afternoons Pete Carlucchi and I play nine-ball at the
Lord Dunsmuir. Pete's only got one hand, so he has to stand
sideways at the table and lay his left forearm down behind the cue
ball for a bridge. If I were making this up he'd be the best nine-ball
player in town. But this is a true story: Pete couldn't pocket a ball
in a peach basket.

He lost his hand in the Number Ten mine under the lake in 1946.
He was sick one day, he'd been up all night with the flu. Number
Ten was a gassy mine and by ten o'clock Pete was having trouble
breathing. He had to stop drilling every once in a while to throw
up. The fireboss started to curse him out, said he'd rather have a
Chinaman down there than a puking Eye-Tie that couldn't take a
little hangover. Pete dropped his rock drill and said he'd better go
find a stinking Chinaman then.

He just walked away from the face, but by the time he got to the
foot of the slope he was choking, stopping every few yards to heave.
Then he passed out. When he woke up the mules were hauling past
him and his left arm was under the wheels of the coal cars. The
mules kept going. When all the cars were past, Pete picked up his
hand from between the rails and ran to the top of the slope with his
left hand in his right hand and the stump of his left wrist swinging
at his side, pouring blood over his trousers and boots.

The foreman and a teamster wrapped his arm in a shirt and threw
him into the back of a wagon. Of course Pete was out cold by this
time. He woke up when they were carrying him into the hospital at
town. He lifted his arm up and looked it over and then he started
yelling Jesus Christ I lost my effing hand.

So the foreman held up a gunnysack and said no you didn't Pete I got it right here.

I break and then Pete steps up sideways and sets his left forearm down gently flat on the felt and bridges on that and gives the cue ball a good hard whack. Since this is a true story nothing falls.

A pack of Players Light. And one of those Big Turks.

Anything else?

What about those peanuts there? I mean are they any good or what?

I don't know. They're barbecue. I'm allergic.

I never heard of anybody that was allergic to peanuts.

Just the barbecue ones. Barbecue sauce, barbecue chips, anything barbecue.

Yeah? What happens?

My lips swell up. I start to cry and my eyelids itch. So, you want some?

I guess not. I bet you got a boyfriend or something.

Three-fifty for the smokes, and seventy-five's four and a quarter. So twenty-five, fifty, and seventy-five's five. Husband. Jerry McKay.

Don't know him. I'm from up-island.

Well, you'd know him if you lived here.

Uh-huh. Listen, where do you get a beer in this town?

Pub's right down the street.

So that's where you and Jerry McKay go?

Right.

You ever go without him?

Are you just trying to keep in practice or something?

No, no, I'm interested. Really.

Everybody in town's afraid of him.

Is that so?

He's a psycho. He likes to beat on people.

I bet that's why you married him. For protection, I mean.

Something like that.

Hey, does that pinball machine work?

No. There's a Pac-Man at the pub. Down the street.

So how'd you meet this psycho anyway?

The first time he got married, I caught the bouquet.

So they come into the Broadway Café, this perfect couple. He's got the button-down and the pleats and important hair. He looks like a man of substance as they used to say. She's an earth-mother type, denim from neck to ankle and serious brown boots. All I can see of her hair is a glossy black band high across her forehead. The rest of it's wrapped in a red-and-white bandanna. Where the bandanna's knotted at the nape of her neck rides a heavy bundle of red-and-white-covered hair. A few strands have escaped from the bundle and the light coming in through the front window catches those strands floating around her like we're all in some movie.

They get their cheesecake, Grand Marnier for him and hers is Amaretto, and they both have raspberry sauce and café au lait. I watch them trading tastes. They don't feed each other, they are mature and decorous people, but the way she slides her fork edge-first through his dessert makes me hungry just watching. It takes them a hell of a long time to eat, and when they finish they get refills of coffee. Her mouth leaves no stain of lipstick on the white pottery mug.

It's clear that they've settled in for a while, there's no way I can outwait them. One of the things I've lost lately is patience. So I fold up my newspaper and leave money on the table and try to slide sideways out of the café.

She sees me anyway. He looks up, curious at the recognition in her look, and I am frozen, locked between the eyes of this perfect couple. After an hour or two she figures she has to say something.

Ed, she says, this is Paul. From work. Paul, my husband Ed.

He looks me over. There are times you just have to be brave, so I stick my open, empty hand out in front of me. Glad to meet you, Paul, I say.

Later the other, the boy, came along, but at first it was only the girl. She didn't knock, just stood on the front step turning and turning the rattly doorknob until I had to get up and see who it was. She was a little straggle of a thing, her clothes looked like rags. Said she had to use my bathroom. I poked my head out the door to see if some houses had sprung up while I wasn't looking. There weren't any others, how could I refuse her? Not another bathroom for miles that I could see, so I pointed the way for her. Into my house, my bathroom. Maybe she was fifteen or twenty. How do you tell these days?

She was in there quite a while when the boy came. She's in the bathroom, I said. He went in there, with her, and I heard the door lock behind him.

I went outside for a minute, just to smell the air. Still no houses, and no cars either. I don't know where they came from. It was getting dark, the sky was sort of purple-grey and smoky. Though I couldn't see any chimneys. If somebody came by I could say, Hey, my kids are here visiting me. Just walked in from someplace, been away a long time. Who'd know the difference? I'd introduce you, I'd say, but they're in the bathroom right now. My daughter and my son. Stop in and meet them later. If anybody came by.

Truth is, I never saw them before. Those kids in my bathroom, I mean. They've been in there a long time now. Once in a while, when I get up to fix myself a drink or something to eat, I stop and talk at the bathroom door. Listen, I say, if you want some supper you can come out and help yourselves. Or if you want to come out and talk. They don't say anything. I don't mind, I say. Only somebody might come by.

My wife comes home from work one day and says we've got to get ourselves a bed of nails. They're all the rage on the coast. She keeps up with this stuff, which is how we got those crystals a while ago, and the Thai cooking utensils before that. She doesn't steer us wrong very often, though I had to tell her that the green parachute-silk harem pants weren't flattering on a woman of her age.

Anyway I'm a little suspicious about this bed of nails business. I went years without a decent sleep, through the waterbed thing and the futon thing. Then the magazines started to talk about cocooning and my wife went out and got us a Sealy Posturepedic. Put it right in the middle of the living room. We liked that bed so well that we cocooned right through the homeless thing, where you were supposed to go sleep on newspapers over a sewer grate or something.

Now she says that cocooning's out and the homeless thing's out and what we need is a bed of nails. But honey, I say, won't it ruin the Eurodown? She just shakes her head at me. Says that the bed of nails gets you centred, concentrating, restful. I point out that the crystals were supposed to get us centred, and the pyramid too. Now they're just more stuff to be dusted.

She's got her heels dug in about this, though, and the more I think about it the more this bed of nails starts to grow on me. I can see the upside, as we used to say back in our BMW phase. A little restful concentration in bed might be just the thing to get me centred. Plus there's the possibility of veils and saris and some of this Kama Sutra stuff, and there hasn't been too much of that going on in our Posturepedic.

Honey, I say, I guess I could warm up to this idea. She doesn't waste any time. Whips out a four-colour brochure and dials the toll-free number that minute.

I never knew her to be fickle before, but she gave up on that bed pretty quick. Said it made her itchy. And those other practices I was thinking about, that stuff never did come to pass. Fact is, she hasn't been around much lately. I believe she's found some other kind of bed that's more her speed. Like the Magic Fingers at the Travelodge.

I don't mind that too much. I'm used to this bed now, it's been weeks since I even tried to get out of it. If she was to come back now I don't think I could get up to help her with her bags or anything. But I guess you'd have to say I still love her. I know I'll always keep a space for her. Right here beside me.

The mail slides through the door slot and lands on the carpet like a bomb. The cat, which had been asleep on my lap, digs in its back nails and leaps to safety under the couch. I don't blame it. Nothing good ever comes through the mail.

I carry the letters, held carefully away from my body, back to my chair. The mail is dominated by a fat, malevolent yellow envelope sealed with buff strapping tape. I set that aside for later. Maybe this time there'll be good news in the other envelopes, but the big yellow one is serious business.

A postcard from Mazatlan: a burro in shades and flip-flops, reclining on a fold-out lounge chair. Beside the chair is a balloon glass filled with green liquid. On the back of the card is my name, my address, and a message: *Claire has got dysentery or something. Leaving today (Jan 17) for La Paz. See you soon, Love, Angie.* I have no idea who these people are. It is September here.

My Bay account is past due. Service charges, purchases of men's hosiery and sporting goods. The people at the store are very efficient, there's never been a mistake on my account. Sometime when I'm not so tired I'll have to check around the house for hosiery and sporting goods, but for now there's still the ordeal of the mail to get through.

I am invited to join the Rare Books in Facsimile Editions Society, the satisfied customers of the Collectors Guild, my superior credit rating will allow me easy access to cash, goods, and services if I take just a few minutes to complete the enclosed application form. My signature authorizes a Personal Credit Reference check, and this invitation in no way guarantees acceptance. This letter is printed on 100% unbleached recycled paper.

The yellow envelope could be slit open with a paring knife, if I had one, or I could take it in both hands and rip the flap off. But I am cautious: I get hold of a corner of the tape between my forefinger and thumbnail, and peel it away. The adhesive lifts off yellow pulp from the envelope. When I'm finished the tape floats to the floor and lies curled up next to the now sleeping cat. The mouth of the envelope yawns.

There's no letter in the envelope, only a thin paperback novel I loaned to a friend years ago. My name should be written on the flyleaf, but it's impossible to tell for sure. The three open sides of the book have been sealed with more buff tape.

Is it the same book my friend borrowed, or a different copy? Maybe it's a new edition, maybe my name's not written in the book at all. The slick, muscular tape gives no clue. Do the words printed on the bleached pages match the title on the jacket, or are there in fact any words on the pages?

The mail could bury you, you could be crushed under the accumulation of messages it carries. Every day more and more of it tumbles toward you, gathering a greater and greater weight of words as it approaches.

But the shiny, comforting postcard is still there on the coffee table. Somewhere in another country, in a different time of year, Angie and poor Claire are arriving in La Paz, thinking already of home and of distant friends. The message was signed: *Love.* Whoever they are, they'll be welcome here.

What kind of bar *is* this says the drunk at the next table. There's two guys *reading* in here. You're reading and that old guy over there's reading. What kind of bar *is* this where guys sit and *read?*

I don't bother to answer. He's a stranger, what does he know about this kind of bar? Anyway I'm not *reading* and neither is the old guy. We're *studying* is what we're doing.

I'm studying a story, a bad one, with an ending that's screwed up. I'm studying it to find out how it got screwed up and how the writer could have fixed it. This is important. I wrote it.

If the drunk at the next table were a regular he'd know that the old guy is Dermot Grady, retired coal miner, seventy-three, a great-grandfather. He's studying too. He's studying his final divorce decree. Looking for some mistake.

for Ed Dyck

at daybreak   between the legs
of guests who have stayed too long
between the legs of card tables
heavy with gin and cheese and sausage
between the last legs of conversation
wanders one-eyed Jack
the host's cat   bored
probably wishing he could sleep

but when the last guests find the door
and when the host at last
finds his bed   Jack
delicately balanced on hind legs
left forepaw braced
on a table leg   reaches up
his right paw   in a gesture
of innocent grace
and inarticulate longing

snares a piece of sausage and takes off

Two songs for Berryman

1

Poor Henry. Poor, poor Henry's lost his saxophone,
birds don't sing to him no more.
— You is a carrot, Mr Bones,
you needs a scrubbin.
— Henry always sitting at stage-side,
waiting, but Bessie's dead,

all these years, won't sing never no more.
— Easy, Mr Bones.
I am feared you got a problem, bein
you is gettin old. You should buy new specs,
pal, you should trim you beard,
you looks like a ol mop.

—Them birds sing, but don't never
they sing to Henry, and sweet Bessie's dead
all these years, my Lord,
poor sweet Bessie's dead.
— De problem, pal, is you got no majinayshun.
Crank up dat ol Victrola, Mr Bones.

2

Well, sir, this is what it comes to.
Ah yes, the noise of the traffic,
the milkman, choirs, tambourines, etcetera.
Henry needs a blanket,
keep old Puss-cat warm.
— *You is from hunger, Mr Bones.*

— Sweet Mary, we all dance around
our own sweet Mary, her eyes
are like pennies, her hair
is black as a telephone.
— Why does you, Mr Bones, allus believe
what you is sayin?

— *I saw nobody coming, so I went instead.*
— Easy, Mr Bones. It's a long walk,
it's a slow strut behin dat box
an de trumpets be shakin de air like crazy.
— Henry can't find his horn, how can he play?
— When we comes to dat bridge, pal,
         we'll cross it.

the child bends to the side   starts to fall
then springs into a catherine wheel
    she rolls across the schoolyard
in spiked divisions of movement

    I know what would happen if she fell
twisting   fragmenting the angles of her body
    I too have bones inside me
but I don't think they can get out

    my joints speak to me in thin
arthritic voices   the child falls
and for an instant   before the packed gravel
opens her knee
all her bones are outside her

children are silently riding the arcs of their swings
or climbing through cages of iron bars   mazes of tires
speaking with hands and the movements of bodies

but one who is running with arms outstretched   wheeling
through sandpiles and leafpiles   is hollowly shouting
in language without modulation or meaning

his throat is a vibrating column of air
and his arms are the silvery wings of an airplane
that cuts through the sky with a roar in this stillness

and drops bombs of language that nobody hears

for Kim

Name another poem, another line
by another dead poet. Stone-dead
John Thompson, one called him,

and he is, a dozen years. There are too many
dead poets, too many poems
written for them. Stone diaries.

Too many
Pat Lowther poems,
MacEwen Nowlan Acorn poems.

There are no secrets, John Thompson says,
said. And I feed on his lines
like any carrion bird.

Kim says the name
of one still ruthlessly alive.
Arguing against suicide, disaster, heart

failure. If you die
she says, that one will write
some stinking poem to your name.

for Dolores

I'm living on an island now. You're still
in Saskatoon, writing your radio poems. I think of you
sitting in a hidden room, a closet under back stairs,
with your headset on, adjusting dials, transcribing

coded messages in your own private code.
The Resistance. Listen, I want to tell you,
do not listen to the radio. It's a trick,
it's all propaganda. Both sides

are lying and you cannot win. I live on an island,
I know about the radio. Something
gets disturbed, gets lost, translated
into languages we don't understand, codes

we haven't learned. High above the ocean
or the prairie something is happening
that turns it all to lies. I'm waiting
for someone to kick down our doors.

in memory of Ken Ho

The camps were worse than prison, every day
I thought I would go crazy. Once I almost killed a man
over a litre of water. But finally the Sisters came.
They said the New World would be like Heaven.
I would have a house, a job, and my daughters
would go to Catholic school. I am Buddhist
but my daughters were very happy.

You understand in my country I was a big man.
After the navy I managed a Michelin plantation.
I had good pension money. We moved to the city
and bought a hotel. I had a Mercedes,
very good car. Saigon was beautiful at night.
There were blue lanterns in front of our hotel.
You could buy anything there.

The Sisters said it would be like Heaven.
I dreamed of blue lanterns, a new hotel
where all the big officers would come.
But at the airport it was so cold, nothing
smelled alive. We had no warm clothes
and the air froze my breath. I couldn't move.
My daughters had to drag me to the car.

for Kate

The faces of women long dead, of our family,
unremembered, existing only in photographs:

that one, thin as a blade, a face you could fold
between the leaves of a book to mark your place,

or that one, standing grim behind her grim husband:
a mouth like Mr. Punch's splits her face.

Our sister painted a portrait of one dead twenty years
and had to invent a smile, no photograph showing one.

They stand in these photographs behind their husbands' chairs
and show no more intimacy than a niece or cousin might,

no more life or humanity than any useful tool.
But there is one, a bit mad perhaps,

in the middle of a family portrait, who has moved her face
resolutely away from the camera and blurred the image.

In an age of heavy tripod cameras and enforced stillness
she erased herself from the family record.

*What I'm trying to describe is that it's impossible to get out of your
skin and into somebody else's. And that's what this is a little bit about.
That somebody else's tragedy is not the same as your own.*

- Diane Arbus

1

There's nothing, nothing
I can do for you. I'm here
only to observe. Your face
has become thin, you haven't washed
your clothes. I don't mean I disapprove
or approve. It's only what I see.

Yes, I remember the way you once were, but that
isn't important. I won't judge
your morals, your psychology, the way
you turned your face, just then, to the window.

I have plenty of film. The light's good.
Now: tell me your story.

2

Your hands are shaking. I notice
that you find it difficult to mount the lens.
I like the silver umbrella you've set above
and beside me, a little cloud on my shoulder.
Do you see the way my eyes catch the light
when I turn my face, like this?

I was so perfect, years ago, it made you afraid.
Now I can sit here in my old clothes,
my old skin, those times past now
and ready to be forgotten.

Why is your face so pale behind the camera?
Tell me: what do you see?

Sometimes at night I walk these harmless streets
wearing the costume of an evil soul.
But I am not what you think
I am when you see me on your sidewalk,
in your backyard, when you see the glint
behind the hedge, your bedroom lamp
reflected in my eyes.

I only want
a little corner of your life. Even when
I stand before the trusting, well-lit
curtainless screen of your living-
room window and see absolutely nothing
going on, I am happy.

Your life is a movie with no soundtrack
but the cars passing and birds and sometimes
far away the sound of an ambulance.
It may be anger or desire
that makes you cry out in your bed.

The windows that close you within
your world and me without are the frames
and mirrors and proscenia
that let me share your love and hatred
and loneliness, that even if you do not know it
let you share mine.

This angle between the avenues of darkness:
where the world has stopped its
stupid turning for a few minutes, an hour,
long enough for coffee and a newspaper,

where the counterman is king of his small
bright corner of the night, can bring you
free coffee, free sandwiches — Go ahead, pal,
I'd just end up throwing them out anyway

— or show you the door when you ask
for another refill. Outside: where the streets
aren't lit and there's no one to pass you
the want ads when he's through with them.

In the middle of the night you pull off the highway
and drive a few miles down a gravel road,
then turn again. Finally you stop in an approach
and sit in your car in the absolute darkness

somewhere in the middle of the country.
You roll the window down and feel
how cold the night is. There are no lights nearby
or in the distance, no farms, no

comforting panels of back-lit plastic bearing the names
of franchise gas stations or convenience stores,
there is no wind and the dark fields around you
are silent. You turn the radio on and are connected

instantly to human voices calling from cities
you've never seen. I want to know
what the best American car is, one says,
and a few minutes later another voice complains

that Orientals are taking over his daughter's school.
Something has to be done, he says, and you nod,
not because you agree but because his is one
lonely voice entrusting his fears and his anger

to the same night, the same starless sky
that endlessly moves and changes above you.
You wonder how many voices
have not got through, have been lost

somewhere between satellite stations,
microwave transmission towers, the humming collectors
of human thoughts, human impulses. Somewhere
in the middle of the country, in the middle of the night

you sit in your car and watch the green
brilliance of your radio dial, the only light
in your world this instant, that simple human light:
tiny and bright and absolutely alone.

The night requires no blessing
and gives none. Throw a stone at it:
nothing stirs. Wars
do not disturb it, or the small
alterations of human affairs.
Electricity is only a disguise.
If it wants to the night will creep in
anytime and take over.

Sleep, if you like. The night
is busy being the night, the size it is
and the shape it wants to be.